JAKE PERALDO

www.Peachtree17.com

Mountain Arbor
Press
Alpharetta, GA

Copyright © 2024 by Jake Peraldo

All rights reserved. No part of this book may be reproduced or transmitted in any form or by any means, electronic or mechanical, including photocopying, recording, or any information storage and retrieval system, without permission in writing from the author.

ISBN: 978-1-6653-0328-6

This ISBN is the property of Mountain Arbor Press (a Division of BookLogix) for the express purpose of sales and distribution of this title. The content of this book is the property of the copyright holder only. Mountain Arbor Press does not hold any ownership of the content of this book and is not liable in any way for the materials contained within. The views and opinions expressed in this book are the property of the Author/Copyright holder, and do not necessarily reflect those of Mountain Arbor Press/BookLogix.

⊚This paper meets the requirements of ANSI/NISO Z39.48-1992 (Permanence of Paper)

0 4 2 3 2 4

CONTENTS

1
NORTH CAROLINA

15
SAVANNAH, GEORGIA

21
MYRTLE BEACH, SOUTH CAROLINA

29
ATLANTA, GEORGIA

37
MY FIRST HOUSE

43
DENVER, COLORADO

55
"LUCKY" CALIFORNIA

65
THE STORE (PEACHTREE 17)

NORTH CAROLINA

I was born in the Appalachian Mountains, 1991 in a college town where my parents met working at a ski resort while going to school at Appalachian State University in Boone, North Carolina. From my earliest memories I knew my life was unique, having an Italian family, I looked at things differently. My dad's family were stone masons migrating from northern Italy, to the Bronx, and then to settle in West Virginia in the early 1900's.

I mainly grew up outside of Asheboro, North Carolina where there weren't Italians. Growing up in the south of America was challenging but I was lucky to have my little brother Alex, who is four years younger. My parents both owned businesses and watched them for years giving opportunity to people in the area. Living in a rural area with a small handful of neighborhoods, there was a lot of land between houses connected with 4-wheeler trails. Most of my friends' families were very southern and grew up hunting which was pretty much standard with every household, except mine.

At four years old I started exploring the land and meeting friends. By the time I was eight I was hanging out with older kids which might have helped to strengthen my mentality. At twelve we moved up to another neighborhood within a mile away in a much nicer house. It was during that time my dad got my brother and I a few dirtbikes. I remember it was a cold Christmas on Badin Lake in North Carolina at my grandfather's house. My grandfather is and was very wealthy living in multimillion dollar houses he had built working as a CEO for a major furniture company. Christmas Eve we searched the house knowing there were motorcycles somewhere. We eventually found them and probably sat on them for at least a half hour dreaming of all the fun we were about to have. The next morning I remember getting a PS2 gaming console and felt at that moment everything in life seemed perfect.

We were an active family, going on technical rock climbing trips in the Appalachian mountains, endless hiking adventures, and even went to indoor rock climbing gyms in bigger cities. By eleven I was a certified SCUBA diver, which was a few years short of the legal age. I also picked up my boaters license that same year which was also a few years before the required age.

We would go to rock quarries with a group of divers from the dive school in town where my dad held one of the highest certifications, divemaster. The quarries in North Carolina have over 100 feet or higher rock walls surrounding pristine clear blue water with sometimes up to sixty feet of visibility. I don't remember diving lower than sixty feet but underwater was an obstacle course of sunken planes, platforms, and boats. It was also a crazy experience camping there with everyone and staying for whole weekends at a time. We would go to places like Ginnie Springs in central Florida on the Santa Fe River and even dove on an offshore ship wreck off the coast of South Carolina in Myrtle Beach. Ginnie Springs is beautiful, diving in caverns with strong currents of water pushing through the cave systems. The Santa Fe River is dark color but the spring system directly off to the side of the river is crystal clear and as cold as any mountain stream. We did a few night dives achieving my advanced SCUBA diving certification there and years later got the chance to travel back to the area to explore more of the river and its natural springs. This was a fun time in my life giving me a sense of adventure and guaranteed love for the outdoors for the rest of my life.

The simplicity continued for a few years while older friends started getting into cannabis. Around that time my mom and her sister would take me to hippie type music festivals where the love for music and high grade cannabis was formed. My mom was into making pottery and we would go to different festivals selling products as a vendor. I would help her make intricate hemp necklaces with her miniature pottery, shells, and collection of beads. These items sold well and I was able to meet different people from across the country. Even getting to meet and hang out with a few famous country music stars backstage. My aunt stayed with us one summer and remember sometimes going in her car to find the jar of "kind bud". I've always associated the smell to the mountains for some reason.

Starting my seventh grade year as a music loving cannabis connoisseur wouldn't last long. I did manage to play on the football team and make it through most of that school year. Eventually for reasons I don't remember, I finished out this year attending the ISS at the high school where I would ride the bus with my older friends. There was one instance where a ISO police officer put me in a painful arm lock for no reason at all, just showing off. This I'm sure didn't help my attitude for authority as I was going through this change in life. That summer I remember visiting boarding schools, probably because my middle school wouldn't let me back. I went to a two week military school summer camp where I quickly said yes for attending my eighth grade year because of the co-ed living situation and access to cigarettes.

Oak Ridge Military Academy was a very unique time in life. There were people like me from all over the world. We would all get together in a few dorm rooms and have fight nights with boxing gloves through thick cigarette smoke. There I got a lot of respect from older guys for my ability to fight. We would sneak out of school grounds and into town where we would find people to buy us cartons of cigarettes, bring them back and sell them out of our footlockers.

I did take the military style program seriously for a few months but found myself becoming once again insubordinate and smoking cannabis with friends at the school. I remember one instance where

I just didn't want to fall in line and do anymore pushups and that was evident to the battalion commander, Col. Lloyd. I'll never forget him, the very loud middle aged guy who was always yelling at everyone. He went and bought me a fast food meal while I ate it in front of my classmates. I guess he figured my peers would be mad at me, at the time I didn't care at all. Shortly after I would sneak out almost nightly to smoke cannabis and listen to music like Bob Marley or Blink 182 on my MP3, mostly by myself. It was early February when they finally gave me the surprise drug test that landed me in hot water, or should I say cold snow.

For the families that could afford it, if you get expelled they would send you to a two month long wilderness backpacking program in the high desert near Moab, Utah. Shortly after being brought to the airport by my mom, I was off to experiencing a cold like I could have never imagined. I remember the guys in Utah picking me up from the airport and bringing me to a small building in a small town. There they provided me with all the gear I would need to survive outside for the next several weeks. I was blindfolded in an old SUV and driven a few hours or so off road into the remote high desert. The cold air was gripping as the truck came to a slow stop and started seeing two or three bouncing LED lights getting closer and closer to me. These were counselors with their headlamps walking to me. I was handed off and placed outside of the group by a small fire that was made for me to stay warm. Until you were officially a part of the group (which took nearly a week), you had to eat cold beans and rice in a severely cold environment by yourself. They taught me how to start my own fire with strings and sticks to be able to "eat warm". If you didn't, tough love. We would also hike a distance of what I believed was ten to fifteen miles a day.

Again It didn't take long for my stubbornness to kick in and a few days just simply refused to get out of my sleeping bag, mainly because of the cold. We would get a tarp with some rope for shelter and a sleeping bag with a mat. I would daily have to shovel away the snow while making shelter to not wake up wet. I remember one day just completely shutting down on wanting to hike and laid there on my bag while the rest of the group played capture the flag for hours, I guess as punishment. I ended up enjoying the experience in a way, probably because of the like minded people and beautiful environment. Towards spring the weather started changing and there were nightly lightning storms which were terrifying. Everyone's tarp would become disconnected and blown away, except mine because of how "bomb" I would make it. I remember going around with the counselors in the middle of the storms and helping people fix their shelter.

After that experience I came back home to be homeschooled for the remainder of my eighth grade year. During this time I really started smoking often and sneaking out at night to be with friends. By ninth grade I was smoking blunts every morning on the way to school with my senior friends listening to Tupac and the newest rap music. This was an addicting feeling that also wouldn't last long. I would stay out at night and start dabbling in selling cannabis at and around my high school.

I don't remember how exactly but I woke up in a behavioral hospital in Raleigh shortly after my birthday in autumn of 2006. The whole time I was thinking that the drug dealing, gangster lifestyles were cool. There I would talk to people about drugs and occasionally have to fight someone. I'm sure it was because of the fighting and constant trouble that forced me there for over a month. I do remember one guy named Alex who was very open minded and taught me a lot about philosophy. He was telling me about this wilderness program where he came from and surprisingly found out I was going to be going to the same program.

Three Springs Wilderness Program was where I was sent to next and was a troubling experience as well as a life changing experience because of the hiking and camping trips. We would sleep in cabins and be expected to attend daily group therapy meetings. In this program I was nearly uncontrollable. I didn't care about moving up in the group levels and constantly found myself in trouble. I was more relatable to the staff and the few African

American group members with me. For the group as a whole, I didn't have much patience for. Whenever we would get visits home I would not come back in time and definitely didn't hear by the rules for being gone, especially the no cannabis rule. I would come back bragging about everything, laughing at the fact that they were again going to remove me from the group and put me on work detail. Or the "Lynch Mobb" they called it.

Mr. Lynch was the owner of this program in Pittsboro, North Carolina. He was a big country guy who followed you on a tractor pushing a line of what seemed like endless wheelbarrow loads of gravel to a pointless recreation field that will never be used. This work was from 6am - 11pm with the only resting time being when we were eating. I started constantly daydreaming about friends, cannabis, and my life outside of there. Soon enough I made it back to the group and somehow began taking things more seriously. Towards the end of my stay there we would go on weeklong canoeing trips to the Suwannee River in central Florida and also backpacking for a week on the Appalachian Trail in Virginia. I had always gone to summer camps and camping trips with family so by then my love for the outdoors and hiking became solidified. It was around then, nearing the end of spring 2007, that I learned my Family will be moving to Savannah, GA.

Up until that point this was the biggest change to have ever come in my life. While on the Appalachian Trail, towards the end of the week I caught a bad infection on my knee. Once we returned I was allowed to go on a medical leave with my grandparents at Badin Lake. While on the leave I would talk with all my friends on social media or on the phone. When I came back from the leave I was more than happy to tell everyone but was soon reminded that wasn't allowed and again was removed from the group. This time the work detail was digging deep holes in the earth to set up latrines. To my counselors surprise the punishment had little to no effect on me and I was happier than ever, thinking about the prospect of a new town, new friends, and going to a new high school.

I was on the work detail for about a week when I was told I was going to be leaving the program early to make the move with my Family to Savannah. I remember my dad driving up the long gravel driveway with his SUV pulling a trailer full of furniture and a few dirtbikes. At that moment I was free.

BACKPACKING IN THE HIGH DESERT NEAR MOAB, UTAH.

SAVANNAH, GEORGIA

The only thing I remember about the drive to Savannah was the hot summer air hitting my skin when we crossed the state line into Georgia. The house was beautiful, in a beautiful neighborhood, and for the first few weeks I was just simply enjoying wearing fresh clothes and listening to Lil Wayne "The Carter" album on my MP3. One of the first nights we went out to eat at this restaurant on the river and remember seeing how many girls were there just hanging out and eager to talk to me. I know I probably looked like a stranger in a place full of preppy collared shirts, plaid shorts, and boat shoes, while I was wearing jeans, tennis shoes, and a fitted cap. On top of that, my vocabulary sounded more like Lil Wayne versus the normal middle class guy from Richmond Hill, GA. To me it was a world full of good ol' boys and beautiful women.

Starting my tenth grade year walking through the halls, I probably stuck out like a sore thumb. I talked to a few people who dressed similar to me, in the hopes I could strike up a friendship or possibly a cannabis connection. One of these days near my locker I met a partly Asian looking guy named Allen who I noticed was wearing similar attire and planned to hang out with him that afternoon.

Because of the past few years being absent from public schools I fell behind in math. I know I tried my best to catch up on everything but besides my best efforts I felt like it would never happen. Our social lives outside of school started evolving and we were still mainly hanging out with older crowds. Coming from a town in North Carolina where I was one of the most popular guys in my school was a big change when coming to Richmond Hill High School.

Everyone loved me here but the people I chose to hang with didn't have the best reputations.

This year we would go to endless house and bonfire parties. Allen and I would find mid-grade cannabis connects downtown Savannah, buy up to a quarter pound, and sell everything to our friends. I knew to never bring anything into school but my lifestyle was quickly overpowering my will to stay and finish school. I wanted to be out in the world on my own and was slowly making that happen. One of the parties we attended was in a carriage house attached from his family's main house; I became friends with the host of the party and was able to move into the carriage house for some months before deciding to drop out of high school.

When my parents moved to Savannah we opened a franchise sporting goods store on the southside of Savannah. I would work there on and off helping manage the store, purchasing inventory, working the cash register, and paying employees. The store was open for almost three years when in 2010 the county slowly worked its way into a recession. We would have problems with employees, amongst other things, that led us to having to close the business. At the time I was much younger and didn't have the mindset to help take things over to try to prevent it from closing. I learned a great deal from the business and successfully planted a seed in my head to grow my own retail store in the future.

The next year was a blur, smoking endless blunts, listening to Gucci Mane, and finding parties downtown. I was seventeen when I was first pulled over in a neighborhood in Richmond Hill for what he said was not fully stopping at a stop sign. We were pulled over half a block from Allen's parent's house where his mom was allowed to take him away. After passing the breathalyzer and field sobriety test, this officer offered for me to take a blood test at the police department which I promptly refused. I had not been drinking and had nothing to hide yet the smell of freshly burned cannabis with the smoke still present was concerning to him. In Georgia in 2009 the cannabis culture was nowhere near to being accepted by anyone and bound to be misunderstood. This was my first introduction to going to jail. Thankfully first thing in the morning my mom was there with a bondsman to bond me out as a one time only deal. I was put on probation for the next year and violated three or four times for dirty urine samples and driving with a suspended license. My probation was reinstated and I spent some months in jail.

MY DAD AND GRANDFATHER IN THE FRANCHISE SPORTING GOODS STORE THEY OPENED IN SAVANNAH, GA.

MYRTLE BEACH, SOUTH CAROLINA

Getting out in 2010 I was feeling pretty much over Savannah and moved to Myrtle Beach, South Carolina where my grandparents on my mom's side lived. I had been going to Myrtle Beach every year of my life and had a deep love for that area. The party scene there was incredible and to me was a major opportunity for distributing cannabis.

Things were going well, I met a girlfriend from Detroit and had a handful of friends until one day my grandmother found a few small bags of cannabis in my laundry and I was promptly kicked out of the house. I did not want to return to Georgia and wasn't old enough or financially stable enough to rent a room somewhere. I stayed with my girlfriend for a few nights and other nights with friends until one day I met a fellow Italian from Boston named Bobby. He was about four years older and a lot bigger than me. Because of my situation, being Italian, and knowing my girlfriend, he gave me an opportunity to stay with him for free at a beach house across the street from the beach. Here I was introduced to the world of serious organized crime, watching Bobby and a few of his friends bring home street bikes lifted from tourists. It wasn't long before the crew had to return to Boston to let things chill out. I was once again at a crossroads and feeling like I was about to be homeless.

Thankfully shortly after I was able to move in with my girlfriend and her family in a nice condo, coincidentally across from where my grandparents lived. I also got a job washing dishes and working as a busboy at a local pancake house. Some time later Bobby returned to the north part of town living in a luxury townhome surrounded by golf courses. My girlfriend and her family were moving to Florida and for some life changing move, I chose to stay in Myrtle Beach and move back in with Bobby. I remember my girlfriend was very upset but for some reason my feelings weren't matched. I was too young and wanted to create my own destiny.

At nineteen I started working at a golf course across the street cutting fairways and was passionate about the work. All the responsibilities that came with being a manager were exciting to me. In the back of my mind I knew this wasn't my calling and would soon be moving on to more troubling and prosperous days ahead.

I would watch gangster movies while Bobby and crew would do their thing at night and ultimately proved to be too enticing to me. By now Bobby moved up to burglarizing local businesses and completely liquidating whole inventories to our living room and garage. Within days the stuff would be gone and replaced with even more expensive stuff. I kept my job and was starting to sell higher grade cannabis but slowly started going on capers with them.

JAKE PERALDO

It was mid to late September when detectives started coming to the townhouse to question us. Somehow we would make a break for it and escape out the back. We would sit on this hill late at night overlooking the police activity while smoking the high grade cannabis I had with me. There was one morning in particular I was home alone and happened to be taking the trash out. The detectives pulled up fast and were talking very aggressively while I played clueless. I knew from the night before that several car trailer loads of things were removed from the house and it was empty. They proceeded to ask me to open the garage, which at first I was hesitant but ended up opening anyway. They bent down in excitement to get the first glimpse of stolen property but were quickly disappointed and left immediately.

I had more money than I had ever saved up in the past and knew I should have, but it was just too hard for me to get across the idea of giving up everything and returning home to Georgia.

One morning I was out working and got a call

from my boss to come to the proshop to fix a leak where I was met with a few detectives and a second degree burglary warrant. They played it cool in front of my boss but as soon as we left the building, I was gone. I remember one guy yelling that he was going to shoot me and I yelled back with, "Please don't shoot me!" I didn't make it far because of the tall fence lines and patrol officers waiting out by the road. Come to find out our heroin addicted neighbor was secretly working with police and providing them with pictures to get out of a DUI arrest one night. There were a few stipulations that prevented me from doing any serious time, mainly the paid lawyer, low criminal history, and lack of being able to identify me on camera. Unfortunately, Bobby was sentenced to a year in prison. I was bonded out by my grandparents for Thanksgiving and got to see Bobby a handful of times before he had to turn himself in to serve his term.

It was getting close to Christmas and I was staying in an older hotel with a room on the beach. I got a call from Allen one night saying I should come back home and that was all the convincing I needed. I had an extremely high mileage, shaky, and older SUV that I knew would not make it back to Savannah. The next day I sold the truck and purchased a 1998 car for around five hundred dollars. A new tire and full tank of gas and I was ready to take the trip back to my life in Savannah. Buying and selling cars was nothing new to me and was probably on my twentieth or so car.

I got home and settled back into life in Georgia but things weren't nearly the same. Most people were off at college and I was at my parents with just the prospect of working construction with my neighbor. I managed to buy a nicer car but that whole year Allen and I were spending all of our time working what felt like dead end jobs. Towards the end of 2012 I was feeling like I needed change. Unfortunately I found out that Bobby died unexpectedly days after leaving prison. Some days later I wrecked my car and had no choice but to stay home. This on top of everything, seemed like the lowest point for me but over the next few weeks some incredible things happened. Alone in my room I would pray to God to send me an angel and help take me to the next chapter in life. I would literally dream at night of my life in exotic places surrounded by new friends.

Thanks to online ads I found a residential contracting company hiring in Richmond Hill. Before starting the job on Monday, Allen and I decided to go downtown on a beautiful Friday night. I remember telling him once we got to River Street that I wanted to talk to the first cute girls we saw. Clearly that wasn't a lie because minutes later we were talking with a few art students debating on where we should all go eat. Little did I know, this girl I just met would be with me for the next three years. We all worked for a few months until Allen and I started talks about moving to Atlanta. For some reason I thought that I would have to leave my girlfriend and make the move with Allen but shortly after breaking the news to her, I found out she was not going to let that happen. The next week she and I took a trip to her dad's beach house in Vero Beach, Florida where she would explain that she wanted to transfer to the art school in Atlanta and help us get a house. Lauren from New York, was my guardian angel at that moment.

ATLANTA, GEORGIA

Sometime early February Allen and I drove up to Atlanta for the weekend to secure a place to live. We quickly realized how much we needed Lauren and called her to come up. We were striking out with everything but somehow riding around with her, we found a perfect little house on the southside of town in East Point. We drove back to Savannah and left my car in the car port of our new house. The feeling of what was soon to be our lives in Atlanta was exhilarating. In East Point we tried to work a handful of jobs but mostly just bought and sold dirtbikes and a few cars here and there. We ended up moving to a nice townhome on Memorial Dr. in Stone Mountain. Here we started making some money with third party installation contracts installing appliances and home workout equipment for major electronics and appliance retailers. Hours were long and work was hard but we stayed persistent. We allowed our friend to move up with us but somehow his job propositions fell through and was becoming a nuisance for everyone to be around.

Eventually Lauren's dad decided to get us a highrise apartment and moved to Northside Drive in Atlanta. Unfortunately Allen did not make the move with us and ended up getting an apartment with our other friend in Stone Mountain. I would still see Allen sometimes but this time in my life was mostly filled with working, making rap beats, and networking with producers. Lauren and I were on good terms but in the back of my mind I wanted to be alone and felt like she would be much happier up north with her friends. Again I was alone in this big city set on trying to make my own destiny. I barely had any cannabis connections in Atlanta and knew I had to go back to Savannah to focus on the herb.

I started taking trips back and forth to Savannah to sell high grade cannabis at my friend David's house. David is at least three years older and has always been there for me when needed. Him and his sister were some of the first people I met in Richmond Hill and credit a lot of connections through them. Going back to Atlanta to get the rest of the stuff from the highrise was a sad day and I would also lose contact with Allen for at least a year. Before leaving Atlanta I stayed in a hotel on the southside for a few days, unsuccessfully selling cannabis. Around this time an inspiring up and coming rapper named Speaker Knockerz died. He lived in South Carolina and most of his videos were shot in Myrtle Beach and Charleston. This inspired me to want to be back in Myrtle Beach and that night secured a nice apartment online.

Over the next year or so in Myrtle Beach I would spend most of my time driving quarter to half pounds of bud back from Atlanta and selling small amounts to different customers I would meet. I ended up moving out of the apartment with my neighbors downstairs from Baltimore. It was winter time at the beach and luxury hotel rates were low. We were able to lease a penthouse suite on the ocean and began working at a golf course again.

I've always felt like I try my best but sometimes I would fall behind on registering my car or reinstating my license. It didn't seem long until I was pulled over and arrested on a slew of misdemeanor charges one day after leaving work. Afterwards there was a "be on the lookout" for me saying I was only there seasonally to sell drugs from hotel to hotel. Feeling stuck in a way and thinking I was treated unfairly, I soon realized the police activity around me was not normal. Not being able to drive, I purchased a moped to get around and of course driving it home from the purchase, they would take me to jail for not having a moped license. The next morning my grandfather bonded me out and after leaving the impound lot I was followed block for block until I made it to the DMV where I would try to get the license. I remember turning around and seeing this same police officer standing at the door with a smirk on his face. I immediately decided against it and in front of everyone accused him of harassment and walked out. Pushing the moped over ten blocks home with my grandfather following me in his SUV, I would be stopped two more times by two other officers. The first said I matched the description of a suspect and needed to see my license, at first I refused. The second told me I couldn't push it on the sidewalk or Ocean Boulevard and had to be on the back street? As he turned the corner expecting me to go to the back street, with a hotel blocking our view, I abandoned the moped and ran to my hotel on the beach.

The city was getting cold but I still had my cannabis and music, mainly listening to Future's "Monster" album and new Chief Keef songs. I walked several blocks every morning before sunrise with ice on the ground to go to work. Most of the time being followed by marked and unmarked patrol cars. We even moved down the road to a more discrete hotel but this wouldn't prevent police from finding our new spot and harassing us with activity in front of our suite nightly.

Somehow I made it through without a major arrest, quit the golf course, and went up to Pennsylvania to visit Lauren in her new college. I've driven to upstate New York and New York City once with her while living in Atlanta and it was one of the best experiences I've ever had in my life. The differences to the north and south are night and day and seemed like I was entering another world every time I drove up. The idea of wanting to be in a bigger city would stay with me for the long haul. Even though Lauren and I were on good terms we knew things would never fully work out.

Not knowing where to go or what to do next I decided to move back up to North Carolina and move in with a friend I knew from high school in Georgia. The city was Greensboro and not far from where I grew up in Asheboro. My grandparents on my dad's side live in the area and it was nice to be close to them. We rented a cheap house that needed updating but I was mainly happy to be back in North Carolina.

I was there for about six months, not really working at all except with cannabis to pay the bills. It was getting close to 2016 and again I started missing Savannah and all my family and friends. With my town car on its last leg from all the trips to "re-up" on herb, I again purchased an older car, sold the towncar, and made my way home.

ALLEN HANGING OUT IN FRONT OF OUR HOUSE IN ATLANTA.

MY FIRST HOUSE

I had always known since an early age that I wanted to own real estate but was currently trying for at least four years to make that happen. The first few days back in Savannah I stayed with my friend Trey. He owned his own construction company and because of his father, was heavily immersed in the world of real estate investments. With a few thousand in my pocket I was set on trying to make my first deal, surely Trey would know someone. Without hesitation he had someone in mind and gave me the number for an extremely successful local investor. The conversation was brief but ultimately I was given a few addresses to check out. It was January eighth and with only a walk around the property, I chose the first address. The feeling was incredible and I knew this was a pivotal moment in my life. The house has three bedrooms on the east side of town and after a few weeks I updated it with some friends to a pretty nice condition. A few friends came to stay with me and once again life was well.

Around April one weekend I got a call from Trey to come deliver some cannabis to where he was staying on Tybee Island. Not having much going on and taking a day off from the girl I was currently talking to, I made my way out to the beach. It's funny how things can happen which will put your life into a whole other direction. I was followed by a police officer onto the island driving my clean sedan I had just recently bought but fortunately was not pulled over. When I got to the lavish beach house wearing my favorite track suit and tennis shoes, I found out this was more than just another cannabis deal.

Trey was there with his girlfriend and her friend Lyndsey. Lyndsey was a few years younger than me and previously knew her from high school. I never expected before driving out there that we would be together for years.

By the end of the year I was able to rent a luxury apartment on the other side of town in Berwick for us and rented my house out to friends for the extra income. For a while I had almost forgotten about the cannabis and was just simply enjoying being with her everyday. I was barely smoking, attending church, and started working with Allen again installing appliances. We would go play golf several times a month and thinking about it all now, this might have been the happiest I'd ever been in my life until then. Our work soon turned into a profitable contracting company and was blessed with successful commercial and residential construction jobs. With our LLC, a few guys, and two trucks, we worked for almost a year.

We would all take trips to the mountains to go skiing and Lyndsey and I would even go visit our grandparents at their homes in North Carolina.

There was one night in particular where her mom was at the apartment and some type of argument ensued between them. They both ran outside quickly with her mom taking her dog. Not thinking of running out and chasing her, I received a call from her about fifteen minutes later saying she got in a wreck in front of my parent's neighborhood in Richmond Hill. Thankfully she was fine but her car was totaled and afterwards I would not see her for almost another six months. I had no idea that this night would again start to change my life. Everytime she called my heart would race but not knowing when the next call would come I grew depressed and restless. Alone at night in the apartment watching movies like "Blow" with Johnny Depp, I couldn't help but to see the similarities in my life.

The restlessness grew stronger and anxiety over Lyndsey turned into motivation to see new places. With thousands of dollars in my pocket and the story of George Jung (the real life character from the movie "Blow") constantly in the back of my mind, I took my truck cross country in search of a real cannabis connection. George Jung at this time was a elderly Bostonian, ex-convict, living in California with an amazing story chronicling his career as a professional cannabis, then cocaine smuggler. The highs and lows of his life were extremely appealing to me. The way he chose his own path, simply for the excitement of doing whatever he wanted to do in this world was intriguing.

DENVER, COLORADO

The next morning I was up early and drove as far west as I could. I woke up in a midwest hotel in Missouri with the idea of going to Colorado to score some cannabis. I made it there within three days and already found half a dozen suppliers online. I was able to weed out the bad and found two legitimate connections. I negotiated for my first pound and met one of the guys "runners" in the parking lot of a local fast food restaurant. The deal was refreshingly pleasant and the hippie type guy with dreadlocks about my age was as nice as could be.

All I ever knew how to move herb was to drive with the product and thought that any other way was too much of a risk. I wish I had a logistical change of heart sooner but I've never been one to regret anything. Here I was back in the world of cannabis distribution and happy to be working with higher quantities and qualities. Over the next few months I took handfuls of trips making more and more money each time.

One cold November morning driving through Kansas I was pulled over, for what my opinion was no reason at all. From my interstate traveling experience, I knew this state trooper was going to search my vehicle and find the bud. Instead I proceeded to cut open the vacuum seals and scattered it out of the window and onto the side of the highway. It was blatantly obvious to him as I slowly came to a stop. He waited for backup then continued with the felony arrest. As I layed down in the tall damp grass at gunpoint while the other officer picked up as much as he could, I knew this was once again another turning point in my life.

PEACHTREE 17

That day my father bonded me out of jail and I was given a misdemeanor charge for the little over three ounces they found. Unfortunately I completely blew off this charge fully expecting to never set foot in Kansas again, come to find out life doesn't always work as expected.

I came home with a strict policy and knew I would never put myself in a situation like that again. I was nearing the end of my lease at the apartment and took a few months off to help rebuild my confidence in the industry. I moved back into my house and inevitably started making more trips. This time after extensive research, I took the risk and found a new way to get my inventory. This worked well but I still had to find a way to not have to take the trip out there. The guy I was purchasing from was the "runner" from my first deal. I got into Denver late one night and made my way to his apartment where he explained to me that I needed to trust him and send him the money. The next deal we did just that and for a few months I got the taste of a real profitable cannabis business. Lyndsey came back to town and I would stay with her in nice hotels downtown on the weekend but by now my priorities shifted more towards my business than to move back in with her.

It was around May 2018 when I started to notice the presence of police, almost seven months after neglecting my Kansas court dates. We were bombarded with weekly visits to the house where I would run out of the back door at the last second. Lyndsey would tell me her stepdad was hearing through his connections that I'm being investigated by the Chatham Narcotics Team but they never secured a warrant to come inside. One day while going to get some food, I was pulled over in a grocery store parking lot on Victory Drive and was surrounded by marked and unmarked SUV patrol cars. In my mind I completely forgot about the Kansas situation and expected them to say I sold a product to an undercover. Sitting in the back of the patrol car I was somehow happy to hear this charge was out of Kansas and for possession with intent to distribute.

Within the next week I was extradited halfway across the country, which was probably the toughest experience I've ever had in my life. I was given a hundred thousand dollar bond and ended up spending almost six months in a few central Kansas jails. Everyone I met there treated me well and ended up becoming friends with a few people. I remember a few times laughing harder than I'd laughed in a long time. During this time I would strategize about how to brand the cannabis and get a dispensary. Because of my operation before getting arrested, hiking in the mountains, and wanting to explore the country, these thoughts were all that raced through my mind the whole time.

The Kansas experience was a tough place in time, it was never certain when my final court date would be as the judge would constantly extend the sentencing date. The day I was released I was sick to my stomach thinking up until the last second if I'll actually be released.

It was a cold, mid October morning with a few inches of snow on the ground. With only the short sleeve shirt, shorts, and thermals from jail, I made my way across the town of Salina, walking to check in with the probation office and find my hotel for the night. From some talks in jail and with my attorney, I half way expected not to be able to leave for a few months. As I walked into the heavily secured probation office I handed the lady's my Georgia ID through the bulletproof glass, they looked at the ID and then back at me with confusion. I guess they don't see too many people from Georgia. Within a few minutes one of the guy officers walks out, sits down beside me in the corner of the room, and calmly asks how I'm doing and what he could do to help. I was not expecting this reaction at all and within seconds was reassured that I can travel home to Georgia today. I left the office almost in tears as I crossed the street to an old shopping center to pick up a wire transfer from my dad.

Because there were no airports, I was forced to wait a few days for a bus. For some reason I wanted to walk the three or four miles to Highway 70 where the bus would be stopping. While in jail one night watching a video music awards show, I saw a live performance from this new artist from Chicago named Juice Wrld. I knew from his cadence, sound, and lyrics that this was the ultimate new era emo/hip hop style artist and quickly ran to my bunk to write his name down. While in Salina I was able to upgrade my phone as my old phone was not turning on due to being off for so long. During my few days in town and on my walk to the bus stop, I would listen to two Juice Wrld songs at least fifty times over. "I still see your shadows in my room, can't take back the love that I gave you." These lyrics were intoxicating to me as I knew two other artists similar to this style had died this year.

With my hair abnormally long and only a manilla envelope with paperwork in tow, I climbed up on the bus to begin my journey home. The trip took at least three days, stopping in St. Louis and Tennessee. I watched someone get arrested for what I thought was drugs and almost witnessed a few fights. The drive into Atlanta and then into Savannah had me finally feeling at ease after almost six months being away from home. Riding down Hwy. 16 and into downtown Savannah where one of my friends was there waiting on me was a feeling that is hard to explain with words. One of my first calls outside of jail was to my supplier and knew I wanted to pick up right where we left off.

Coming back home to live with my parents on probation was something I wasn't used to. By then I was twenty seven and had nearly spent the last ten years on my own. I doubt they agreed or approved of my lifestyle but ultimately they trusted me and allowed me to work out of the house. While in jail in Kansas I came up with the brand name "Peachtree" and after being released, made a logo with stickers and then put them onto mylar bags. Traffic in and out of the driveway was heavy and soon had to start meeting people down the street or even go on the occasional delivery. For the first few months I played by the rules of probation and wasn't smoking, until I learned there wouldn't be any urine samples. By now I was finished with tobacco and blunts altogether and would only roll up king sized natural cannabis papers. Nearly every morning I would step outside, listen to underground Baltimore/ DC rappers, smoke, and plot my day ahead.

I would also listen to podcasts and documentaries online. One in particular was with a major figure in the legal cannabis industry named Berner and his talks with the famous godmother of cocaine, Griselda Blanco's son, Micheal Corleone Blanco. Once again the conversation was inspiring and I picked up a handful of game from them, mostly the idea of riding in taxis if needing to drive with wholesale amounts and ultimately Micheals father investing in gold and real estate.

2019 I would drive to places like the tip of Maine, New York City, Boston, Key West, California, and even up to Seattle to meet a new supplier I met through my friend David. David was now living in Arizona and would also take trips to see him and his wife in Mexico.

With my ample freetime and seemingly infinite

budget, I started to visit my brother more. He had just graduated college at the University of Georgia and helped him move out to Denver, Colorado. In the past our lives were always drastically different. Up until around 2012 he didn't approve of me doing cannabis, he was always an honor roll student and all star on every team he ever played for. I believe that over the years he looked at my life and never wanted to make the same mistakes, I was proud of him. We would go on hiking trips in the Rockies, ride bikes around downtown, and go to major league soccer games where he was employed. He ended up transferring his job to a Nashville team and moved to the north part of Nashville, Tennessee. I would always make it a point to come see him. Not long after, he met a girl, fell in love, and moved back to her home town near Sonora, California where they purchased a house to be closer to her family.

MT. KATAHDIN, BAXTER STATE PARK IN MANIE.
NORTHERN TERMINUS OF THE APPALACHIAN TRAIL.

"LUCKY" CALIFORNIA

Around late 2019 I was having problems with getting good quality cannabis consistently and my Washington guy was falling through for multiple reasons. Towards the end of my year and a half on probation I bought a much nicer house from the real estate investor and set out to renovate the entire property. Unfortunately, because of problems with my business, production on the house grew slow as my budget dwindled. Coronavirus was starting to make its rounds online as a meme but nothing serious. My hippie type supplier in Colorado moved back east and once again knew I had to work my connections to find a California supplier. I met a distributor in El Centro, California while staying with David and could only think of reaching out to him. He said he would try but couldn't make any promises.

Some days later he texted me back saying "I'm in good hands." and introduced me to Lucky. Lucky was nineteen, living in Riverside County, and from the looks of it, was a big time supplier teamed up with his twin brother. Because of my experiences in the past with trust issues and not thinking I could get a rental car, I knew I had to drive out there and meet him in person. With maybe three thousand dollars in hand and a compact SUV I bought from my dad, I set out on what was probably my last cross country road trip. I met him on Long Beach, picked out a type of herb, and followed him back to his house in Murrieta. He had a nice house and car, nearly ten years younger, living out west in what was again another world compared to the south. He was a really good guy and got me the best quality he could at seventeen hundred dollars a pound. We talked about our future business plans and how we were going to do this as big as possible.

I felt like my business was saved and over the next eight months I talked to him often. We would text affirmations weekly and the orders were growing larger and larger each time. While out in California meeting Lucky, I drove to places like San Francisco to visit Alcatraz Island and the Golden Gate Bridge.

I remember driving back in early December and staying with Allen's brother at his apartment outside of Atlanta. I woke up with a sore throat and drove back to Savannah with a high fever. By the time I made it home the high fever turned into extreme body aches followed by over a week of an upper respiratory infection. Feeling sicker than I ever had in my life, sitting on my parent's couch one night, the news came across TV that the artist Juice Wrld had died. The news and everything in the moment was too much to handle and I broke down. Days went by and the achy cough was not subsiding. I drove to the closest available doctor I knew, who I recently met through Allen.

Nearing retirement, Dr Waguspac was the coolest doctor I've ever met and would talk to him openly about my life and profession. He advised me I should go to the hospital because I had pneumonia which again, scared me almost to tears. At the height of my symptoms, coronavirus was becoming a threat in America, everything was shutting down and it was evident to me what I had contracted. All I could do was pray and seemingly overnight, I started feeling physically better than ever.

Times were changing and things were more prosperous as I worked to perfect my craft. I was off probation and now back living with Lyndsey and her roommate in a townhome near Richmond Hill in Savannah. I was once again feeling content with life as the renovations on my newest house were nearing completion. I was doing numbers, endless deals in the parking lot of the townhome, back to back, trying to dodge neighbors and maintenance men. I'm sure to everyone it was obvious but with a smile on my face, people couldn't help but love me. I probably had at least two hundred active customers and hundreds of other people that I knew in the area. My prices and quality were developing as some bad news would inevitably make its way back into my life.

One day Lyndsey's dog Rascal, a shih tzu who we both loved dearly, got sick and I knew he would die soon. I think he was thirteen years old but we had a deep connection with this little guy. Around this time my supplier Lucky dropped off the map and wasn't able to get ahold of him. I guess the guy who introduced us didn't know what was going on either. Two weeks later, after researching him consistently, I found a news article online with his name saying he was killed in an altercation. My heart felt for him and I knew I would never forget what all he did for me. Sometime later his brothers contacted me to tell me about what happened. While working with Lucky's brothers, I was once again networking on the side for an even better supplier.

Remembering some weeks prior I was receiving text messages saying I sold to someone who is now working for one of the best cannabis companies in

America. They were telling them about me and wanted to do business. Of course I've heard it all over the years and after several weeks to think it over, I decided to take them up on their offer.

Somehow I managed to rent a brand new white SUV and purchased a round trip flight to Los Angeles. Again I was off to California and looking forward to the biggest deal of my career. We were set to meet on a certain day but for the first few days all I wanted to do was make the drive to see my brother. We would hang out at his house and go ride around looking for difficult mountains to set out and climb. Driving through the hills in California listening to new emo style rap music seemed to put me in a trance as the sights, smells, and sounds were all brand new to me.

On the way into Los Angeles I stopped at the bank to grab some cash and went to a store to pick up all the materials I would need. I made my way to Hollywood where I had to stop at a gas station to meet the few guys that would be taking me to the deal. They were about twenty one and both driving brand new white sports cars as they pulled up next to me, introducing themselves and telling me to follow them. As a convoy we drove a short ways and pulled up to a security booth to what looked like a commercial office complex. We made our way inside and up to a large suite with hundreds of different products. It didn't take us long to work out a deal which seemed like it was specifically pulled aside for me. Everything went smooth and even got a text from one of the guys inviting me to a mansion party in the Hollywood hills afterwards.

The next day I drove back up to Sanora to spend the rest of my time there with my brother before making my way back to the airport.

THE GOLDEN GATE BRIDGE IN SAN FRANCISCO.

MY BROTHER ALEX ON ONE OF THE MOUNTAINS WE HIKED IN CALIFORNIA.

THE STORE (PEACHTREE 17)

It was nearing December 2020 when someone I knew contacted me offering what would be the most profitable venture of my career. Dr. Waguspac was retiring soon and told me it was possible he could get my application accepted from the owners to take over his commercial lease in front of a major retailer on Highway 17. Since my incarceration in Kansas, I was consistently trying to obtain some type of shop where I could focus on legal cannabis. By now CBD cannabis was legal in Georgia and knew this was a way to build a successful brand around something I love.

Negotiations and verifications didn't take long and soon I was set up in a waiting room with my office, display case, workbench, and several pre-packaged products for sale. I couldn't believe how lucky I was to have this perfectly centralized location surrounded by all my clients and couldn't imagine being anywhere else in Savannah. By now I had well over 400 hundred customers. I was working so hard and so long that I even hired a chef to cook and bring me food during the week.

My business was progressing at a fast rate and I was meeting new clients daily as I purchased lights, surveillance systems, and furniture. By now I felt it was the right time to work on my new logo. I previously had the Peachtree logo that a student from SCAD helped me make in 2018 but knew I wanted to go all out on this one. I called a design firm in Los Angeles and started the process for the new artwork. I knew I wanted something different and considering my story, I knew exactly what I wanted it to look like.

The graphic designer was a pleasure to work with,

she was actually a TV star from the 80's who played on "Baywatch". I felt like everything was falling into place perfectly. The suite was an old doctor's office and I knew in the future I would be doing some renovations but this didn't deter me from thriving. Shortly after getting the new artwork in I reached out to a local sign company. A few weeks and about a thousand dollars later and I had a sign out front on the sign monument with my artwork advertising for everyone driving by to see.

I was still growing at a fast rate as a few months went by. The owner of the complex would stop by almost weekly to say hey. His name is Doug, in his 70's and some years ago was the founder of a newspaper based in Savannah. In fact the name of the complex was named after the newspaper. I feel like his legacy is significant being the founder of a popular newspaper and heavily invested in real estate. I was honored to have my first location in the same building.

One day while visiting me, actually the same day I was about to start the first phase of renovations,

Doug was telling me about the T-shirt shop several suites over that had neglected to pay his rent for the past handful of months. Having experience with an eviction in the past at my first house, I knew I could easily make this happen. Although the offer from Doug was clear, I could tell he was apprehensive to let me handle this. We had a writ of possession from the sheriff's department but Doug wanted things to go smooth and not have this guy mad at us. I respected that and knew this was a game changer for my business, ensuring our success as a brand.

As it turned out, the owner of the t-shirt shop is the same guy who helped Allen and I make business cards and signs for our contracting company that we operated in 2017. It didn't take long to find him deep in my emails and contacted him with an offer I knew he wouldn't be able to refuse. It didn't take much, maybe one hundred dollars and that evening he was here to hand over the key. For the next two or three hours my friend JT and Allen helped me change the locks and start cleaning stuff out. Once again, the feeling was incredible and I knew this would be a blessed year.

The next morning Doug stopped in the suite to talk to me. He was unsure if he should be happy or mad as he just saw that the eviction notices were gone and the locks had been replaced. I explained everything and even showed him our emails proving our negotiations. I visibly saw the weight lift off his shoulders, demeanor change, and in that moment I earned a great deal of respect from him.

I started making phone calls to obtain everything I would need to be a legitimate CBD company in Savannah. After years of planning and now having the store, I knew exactly what I wanted to call it, "Peachtree 17". Seventeen comes from the highway the shop is on, which is also a highway I have a lot of history with being the main road that goes through Myrtle Beach, and is also the year I decided to take cannabis seriously as a career. It took several weeks but I was able to get a new LLC, sales tax certificates, and verification online for our own company page. I had a few local wholesale warehouses where I could easily obtain my inventory and was having to order more and more each time. I designed t-shirts with my logos and had thousands of stickers made to freely give away to people. I even hired a few people to help out, especially while I was out of town and began doing more sales than ever before.

Most of this year I would fly to places like New York City, or into Los Angeles to try to find another commercial lease for my shop. I also did a great deal of exploring, hiking mountains, and visiting my brother. I met a bunch of new real estate and clothing connections but chose for whatever reasons, mostly zoning laws, not to sign a lease. Every time I was out of town I would have employees run the shop which was strategic for growth. The customers are from all walks of life, younger, older, and with the positivity I promote on social media we continue to grow.

I was overly happy with everything, making a life out of cannabis, music, and clothing. I could have never imagined at thirteen that this is what I would be doing at thirty. I was getting more respect from my family, friends, and the community. I truly love waking up everyday to help people.

I also want to mention meeting Kristian. At nineteen he is well organized and reminds me of myself. I knew he was much more advanced than me at that age and didn't have to go through quite the same struggles. As our massive clientele merged into one, I felt like he was just as in love with the brand as I am. With his help, online reviews, customers, and ratings started to climb. We became close friends and considered him one of the biggest assets for the business.

By now everyone we interacted with fell in love with us but things were still tough for me in my personal life. In early July I chose to move out of Lyndsey's townhome because we weren't getting along.

The next few months I spent over a hundred thousand dollars renovating the shop and finishing renovating my newest house. The shop was looking nice compared to when I first moved in. Everything was brand new, including a new fish tank and turtle named Clarence. I purchased an ATM and with the help of Allen and Kristian, within a day was receiving money into my business account. I was even able to lease an electronic billboard bringing in dozens of customers a day from people traveling along Interstate 95.

For Thanksgiving my parents and I drove up to North Carolina to see my grandparents. My grandparents on my mom's side, who I was close with, had both passed away the previous year. I spent a lot of time with them in Myrtle Beach when I was younger and can't even begin to explain everything they did for me over the years. We had a great deal of respect and understanding for one another. My grandfather was a Lt. Colonel in the Navy, spending his whole life traveling the world and providing for his family. My grandmother was a caseworker, working with underprivileged kids, and I can still remember her unique laugh to this day.

While in North Carolina visiting my grandparents on my dad's side, I was eager to tell them everything about my business. Even though my life was better than ever, I still felt like I was making sacrifices to live happier in the future.

One day on our Thanksgiving trip I decided to hike Pilot Mountain which is about half an hour away from my grandparents house. The mountain is steep with a hundred foot wall of granite surrounding the peak making it extremely dangerous to summit without ropes. After researching, I learned that a thirty year old woman fell off the wall and died earlier that year. From talks with my grandfather I knew of a spot that used to have ladders where you could access the top but knew I didn't want to take the risk.

Interstate 40 made a turn in the hills and the mountain was in clear view, beaming down on me with a sense of fear and excitement. I was ready for the hike and even said a prayer for safety, professing my love and respect for the mountain. After hiking a little ways on the trail I knew it was going to take too long to summit and chose to go off the trail, working my way straight up the mountain. The hike turned into a climb through thick underbrush inching my way to the top, one calculated footstep at a time. I was feeling way in over my head, reminiscent of dangerous times where Allen and I climbed Stone Mountain in Atlanta, or when my brother and I would tackle fourteen thousand foot elevated mountains in the Rockies.

I finally got to the top where there was a trail encircling the massive rock pinnacle and a service road to take you back down. People were there with their families enjoying the view and having early afternoon snacks. Wanting to rehydrate, I was disappointed to find out the water had been shut off, probably because of coronavirus. I was increasingly frustrated as I walked down the long service road with endless cars passing me.

That night while watching the news with my family, I learned that shortly after leaving the park a forest fire had started and was quickly consuming the whole mountain, including up the one hundred foot wall and onto the peak. Despite me just being there, I knew in my heart I was relieved it wasn't caused by me. The fire burned over a thousand acres and over the next week would constantly research what was going on.

A few days later I got a call from Allen saying our good friend we grew up with died that afternoon from what we assumed was a fentanyl overdose. Once again this was too much for me and I spent the whole night upset and unable to sleep.

I've had a large handful of friends die over the years but this was different. For the past 15 years Aren was a consistent figure in my life. Even though from high school we didn't have the best reputations, we were the same age and he had always been there for me, especially the past year. He spent hours on the phone helping me negotiate with the Department of Revenue and different companies during times when I was just too busy and irritated to calmly handle the situations myself. He would counsel me on how to talk to people and genuinely cared about me and my business. He even helped me renovate the shop with Allen, painting and installing flooring.

I was pretty upset over his death and angry with myself, feeling naive because I couldn't tell he was on drugs. After the funeral I got an opportunity to talk to his mom, emotionally trying to explain how much he's helped me and how much of a good guy he was. He had a large contribution to the success of Peachtree 17 and again I knew this was someone in my life who I'll never forget.

The store is constantly gaining in popularity. Inventory and online views are high and we even mastered the process of producing our own oil cartridges for vaping. I purchased machines and custom cartridges from Chinese companies in Los Angeles and enjoy doing business with them. They tell me how much they love my brand and their level of customer service is admirable.

In Los Angeles I met with a clothing designer in his studio and designed two types of hoodies. One is embroidered with my original Peachtree logo and the other is tie-dye with light blue, green, and white with the new Peachtree 17 logo. In my opinion the tie-dye hoodie and logo is one of my best accomplishments, besides the store.

I look at the store like a blank canvas that can be designed anyway we imagine. I have galaxy projectors projecting colors over our artwork and framed pictures. We have racks of clothing on display and bought a custom retail counter with built in LED lights from Miami. I try to create an environment that people will enjoy for years to come. Peachtree 17 is a place where we can come to learn about people, help them, and express our creativity. There are a lot of different directions we could take the business as we grow but we are determined to stay committed to our customers.

One of these days I was lucky enough to meet a beautiful girl named Nina, who purchased one of our hoodies. Nina is a huge inspiration for me and helps me tremendously with the shop. With her as a major motivating factor I was able to finish renovating my newest house for us and upgrade the shop in several ways. She helped me create new graphics for stickers and t-shirts as well as spending a lot of time painting murals of our logos. She is extremely talented and together we both enjoy using our artistic abilities to create and bring our ideas together.

My life has never been easy but I love every second of it. I realize the leadership position I'm in and work everyday to help uplift family, friends, and everyone who supports us. I truly care about people and the impact I make on this earth.

THE ORIGINAL PEACHTREE LOGO EMBROIDERED ON THE HOODIES.

THE PEACHTREE 17 TIE-DYE HOODIES.

PEACHTREE 17 ELECTRONIC BILLBOARD THAT I LEASED ON HWY. 204 BY I-95.

Dear Jake,

Just a little love from me to you.
You are a man of many opinions
but you are passionate. You are
ambitious. Your talent is
present, just shy of evident and
the world does not yet know what
a fine human being it has shaped.
I know things are not easy, but I
applaud your positivity and your
strive for knowledge, well being
and love!

Lauren
7/14/14

www.ingramcontent.com/pod-product-compliance
Lightning Source LLC
Chambersburg PA
CBHW052150070526
44585CB00017B/2062